making
MARMALADE
SIMONE GOODING

Tuva Publishing

www.tuvapublishing.com

Address Merkez Mah. Cavusbasi Cad. No:71
Cekmekoy - Istanbul 34782 / Turkey
Tel: +9 0216 642 62 62

Making Marmalade

First Print 2020 / June

All Global Copyrights Belong To
Tuva Tekstil ve Yayıncılık Ltd.

Content Sewing

Editor in Chief Ayhan DEMİRPEHLİVAN
Project Editor Kader DEMİRPEHLİVAN
Designer Simone GOODING
Technical Editors Leyla ARAS
Graphic Designer Simone GOODING, Ömer ALP
Abdullah BAYRAKÇI, Tarık TOKGÖZ
Photograph and Illustrations Simone GOODING

ISBN 978-605-7834-05-8

TuvaYayincilik TuvaPublishing
TuvaYayincilik TuvaPublishing

Contents

step inside 7

materials & notions 11

setting the eyes 12

marmalade rabbit 16

spring
dress 24

ear bows 26

chicks 28

butterfly wings 30

summer
apron 36

headscarf 42

basket 44

strawberries 46

autumn
dungarees 52

blouse 54

vest 58

carrots 60

tote bag 62

winter
coat 68

skirt 72

bonnet 76

bedtime
moses basket bed 84

sleeping bag and pillow 88

pyjamas 94

baby bunny 98

templates 105

suppliers 128

stitch little Marmalade Rabbit . . .

and over 20 seasonal outfits and accessories

making MARMALADE

SIMONE GOODING

Step inside...

... the enchanting world of **MARMALADE RABBIT** created by artist and illustrator Simone Gooding.

Containing a mixture of charming illustrations and photographs to help bring beautiful Marmalade to life. In this craft book you will find a variety of seasonal outfits and accessories to stitch and make.

Travel along throughout the year with little Marmalade Rabbit as she gathers all she needs to explore the small world that surrounds her.

You will find a Moses Basket style bed with warm Winter Sleeping Bag and Pillow, Dungarees and felt Vest for those chilly Autumn walks, a Headscarf and Apron for strawberry picking on those lazy Summer days, Felt Butterfly Wings to celebrate Spring... and many more.

With 100% wool hand dyed felt Marmalade Rabbit, and over 20 original outfits and accessories, 'Making Marmalade" provides all the inspiration and know how needed to bring this beautiful rabbit to life.

Materials & Notions

100% wool hand dyed felt

I have been using this wonderful fabric for many years now. It is very strong but also wonderfully soft so performs beautifully every time. I highly recommend you use very high quality wool felt, poor quality or synthetic felt will not withstand the small seam allowance, tight turning of pieces and firm stuffing required.

buttons

For many years now I have been collecting vintage buttons. I just love to use vintage buttons, they have such wonderful colours, patterns and designs. My favourites are made of Bakelite Plastic from the 1950's and 60's. I have used one from my collection on the coat. I also keep on hand a small collection of tiny 6mm (¼") buttons. These are great for small toy clothing as in this book.

English glass doll eyes

I just love this product! They are beautifully handmade and are very easy to use. They are jet black and have a little sheen on them which help to bring your toy animal/doll to life.

setting the eyes

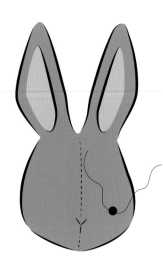

1 Mark the position of the eyes with pins

2 Cut a long piece of Gutterman Upholstery Thread and thread it through the metal loop at the back of the eye.

3 Thread a long doll making needle with both ends of the thread, and push the needle through the front of the face at the position of the first pin. Bring the needle out in the stuffing at the neck.

4 Take the needle off the thread and thread the needle again with only one length of the thread. Push the needle up through the stuffing and out of the face right next to one side of the eye. Repeat with the remaining thread on the other side of the eye.

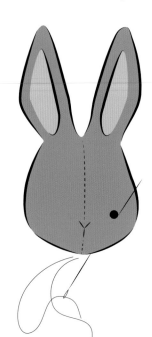

5 Take the two lengths of thread that are poking out on either side of the eye and tie a triple knot, pulling it tight so the knot is hidden behind the back of the eye.

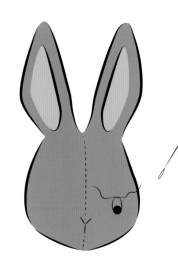

6 Now thread the needle again with one of the lengths of thread and push the needle back in next to the eye and out through the stuffing in the neck. Repeat with the remaining thread.

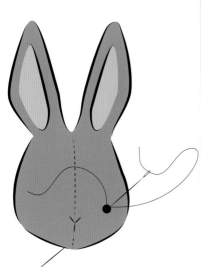

7 Tie a triple knot in the stuffing in the neck a few times until the eye is secure. Repeat steps 1-7 again with the remaining eye.

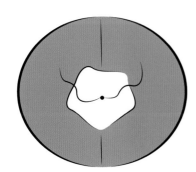

meet Marmalade

marmalade rabbit

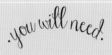

.you will need.

- . 38cm x 26cm (15"x 10") caramel 100% wool felt for rabbit
- . 11cm x 10cm (4½" x 4") cream 100% wool felt for inner ears
- . 5cm x 5cm (2"x 2") white 100% wool felt for tail
- . 30cm (12") pipe cleaner for the ears
- . x2 5mm black English glass dolls eyes
- . Black embroidery thread
- . Toy fill
- . Gutermann Upholstery Thread
- . Sewing machine thread to match the felt
- . Long doll making needle
- . General sewing supplies

* 3mm (⅛") seam allowance included

* templates on page 106

* finished size 26cm (10")

head

1 Machine stitch around the head pieces leaving open where indicated at the base of the head. Leave the dart at the back of the head open at this stage.

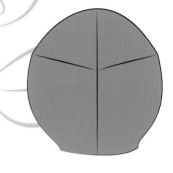

2 Position the gusset at the back of the head so that the seams match, machine stitch the gusset from edge to edge, turn right side out, making sure to gently ease out all the curves.

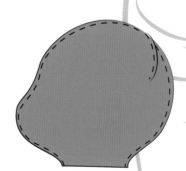

3 Stuff the head until very firm with toy fill. The head circumference should measure approx. 19cm (7½")

face

1 Mark the position for the eyes with pins. Following the eye setting instructions on page 12, attach the English glass eyes.

2 Using 2 strand of black embroidery thread, stitch two tiny back stitches either side of the pointed nose and one longer back stitch down the seam in the face as the mouth.

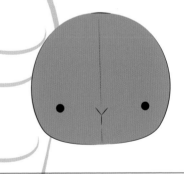

ears

1 Cut two ears from cream felt and two from the same colour felt as the body. Place them together in pairs each pair having one cream and one body colour.

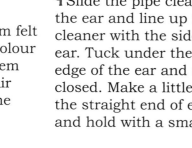

2 Machine stitch all the way around each ear leaving open where indicated, turn right side out, leaving the bottom straight edge open.

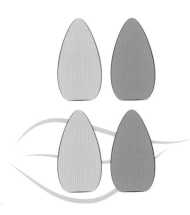

open

3 Cut approx. 15cm (6") length of pipe cleaner and fold it in half, gently mold the long sides of the pipe cleaner so they take on a slightly bowed 'V' shape.

4 Slide the pipe cleaner inside the ear and line up the pipe cleaner with the sides of the ear. Tuck under the raw open edge of the ear and stitch closed. Make a little fold in the straight end of each ear and hold with a small stitch.

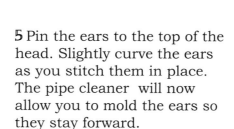

pipe cleaner   stitch

5 Pin the ears to the top of the head. Slightly curve the ears as you stitch them in place. The pipe cleaner will now allow you to mold the ears so they stay forward.

body

1 Machine stitch all the way around the body pieces leaving open where indicated at the back, leave the gusset at the base and top of the body open at this stage.

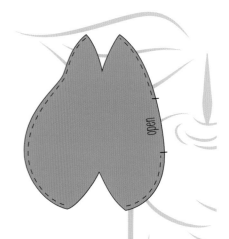

open

2 Position the gusset at the base of the body so that the seams match, machine stitch the gusset from edge to edge, repeat with the gusset at the top of the body.

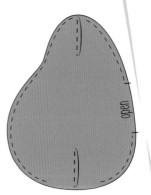

open

3 Turn right side out through the opening in the back, making sure to gently ease out all the curves and points.

4 Stuff the body until very firm with toy fill, Hand stitch the body closed tucking in the raw edge as you stitch. The circumference around the middle of the body should measure approximately 20cm (8").

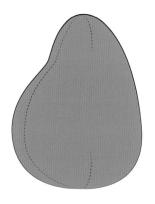

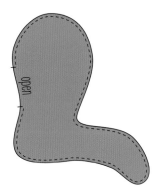

5 Make a little hollow in the stuffing in the head and push the top of the body inside the head opening quite firmly, making sure the neat seam on the front of the body lines up with the front of the head. Place pins in to hold tight while you stitch the head on to the body, stuff a little more as you stitch if needed so the head is firmly attached.

2 Turn right side out and stuff the whole leg well. Hand stitch the leg closed tucking in the raw edge as you stitch. Repeat with the remaining leg.

arms

1 Stitch the arms all the way around, leaving open where indicated.

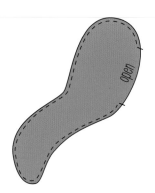

legs

1 Cut out four legs from matching felt. Place two legs together and stitch all the way around the leg and foot leaving open where indicated at the back of the leg.

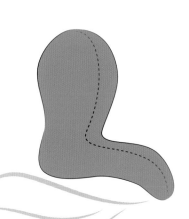

3 Pin the legs in place on each side of the body, and with two strands of Gutermann Upholstery thread and a long doll making needle, stitch right through one leg through the body and out the other side of the other leg, keep going through in this fashion many times until the legs are firm, fasten off.

2 Turn right side out and stuff the arms firmly, close the openings on the arms.

3 Pin the arms to each side of the body just under the head and with two strands of upholstery thread and a long doll making needle, stitch right through one arm through the body and out the other side of the other arm, keep going through in this fashion many times until the arms are firm, fasten off.

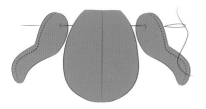

tail

1 Using matching thread to the felt gather by hand around the outer edge of the tail circle. Pull up the gathers so there is a small opening and fasten off but do not cut the thread yet. Stuff the tail until quite firm.

gather

2 Now stitch around the gathered circle again and pull the gathering until the opening is closed a little further.

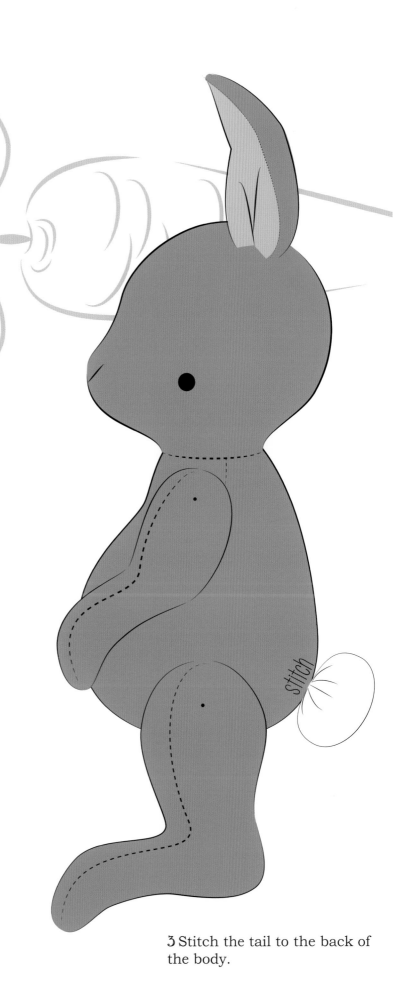

stitch

3 Stitch the tail to the back of the body.

Spring

dress

1 With right sides together, place the dress fronts together and machine stitch all the way around, leaving open where indicated along the side edge. Clip the corners and curves and turn right side out, hand stitch the opening closed and press well.

2 Take two of the dress back pieces and with right sides together, machine stitch all the way around, leaving open where indicated along the side edge. Clip the corners and curves, turn right side out, hand stitch the opening closed and press well.

3 With the two remaining dress back pieces, machine stitch down the centre back seam, open out and press. Using a matching Perle thread, Stitch two small button loops.

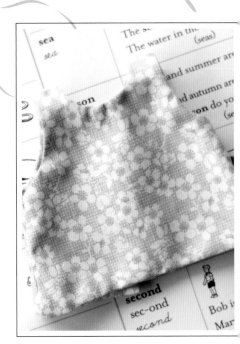

4 Now machine stitch the rest in the same way as for step 2.

two finished dress backs

5 Hand stitch one dress back to the dress front along the shoulder seam and down the side seam. Repeat with the remaining dress back.

6 Stitch two 6mm (¼") buttons in place on the back opposite the loops.

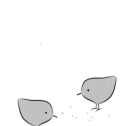

ear bows

you will need.

. 30cm x 10cm (12"x 4")
  fabric for bows
. 10cm (4") thin elastic
. General sewing supplies

✳ 5mm seam allowance
  included

1 For the bows cut the following:

X2 pieces that measure 5"x 4" for the bows

X2 pieces that measure 2"x 1" for the middles

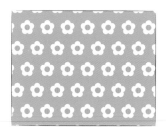

x2

x2

3 Tuck in the raw ends and press, bring the long bow strip ends together and hand stitch them so you have a ring.

4 Gather the centre of the ring, pull the gathers tight and fasten off.

2 With right sides together, fold each bow piece in half lengthwise and stitch down the long side, leave the ends open. Turn right side out and press the seam into the middle.

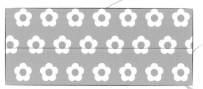

5 Take the middle piece and press the long raw sides in to the centre, wrap the bow middle around the centre of the bow and hand stitch in place.

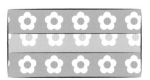

6 Cut approx. 5cm (2") of thin elastic and thread it under the back of the bow middle. Hand stitch the elastic ends together.

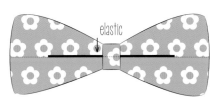

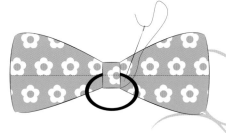

chicks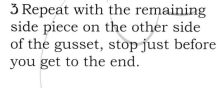

... you will need!

- 10cm x 10cm (4″x 4″) yellow wool felt for each chick
- Black embroidery thread for the eyes
- Orange embroidery thread for the beak
- Embroidery thread to match the felt
- Toy fill
- General sewing supplies

* templates on page 107

1 Using two strands of matching embroidery thread, place the two chick side pieces together, blanket stitch along the top edge.

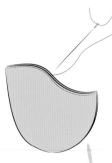

2 Blanket stitch one side piece to the gusset piece, matching the symbols.

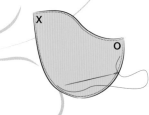

3 Repeat with the remaining side piece on the other side of the gusset, stop just before you get to the end.

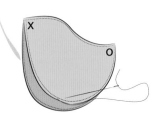

4 Stuff the chick until firm, continue stitching to the end. Fasten off.

5 Using two strands of black embroidery thread, stitch two French knots in place for the eyes.

6 Using two strands of orange embroidery thread, stitch over and over on the pointed end to form the beak.

7 Make as many chicks as you like, four fit snuggly in the basket.

butterfly wings

- . 15cm x 12cm (6"x 5") peach felt for wing set A
- . 15cm x 10cm (6"x 5") tangerine felt for wing set B
- . 12cm x 6cm (5"x 2½") aqua felt for small dots and flowers
- . 12cm x 5cm (5"x 2") coral felt for teardrop
- . 7cm x 7cm (3" x 3") white felt for large dots
- . Small scrap of black felt for tiny dots
- . Embroidery thread to match and contrast the felt
- . 60cm (24") of thin velvet ribbon
- . General sewing supplies

✷ templates on page 109

1 Lay out the two wing pieces from set A. Pin in place the decorative teardrop shapes and small dots. Using two strands of matching embroidery thread, blanket stitch around the shapes. Using the diagrams as a reference, add decoration with back stitch and French knots in contrasting thread colours. Using two strands of black embroidery thread, stitch a French Knot in the centre of the tiny dots to hold them in place.

2 With wrong sides together, and using two strands of matching thread, blanket stitch around the outer edge of butterfly wings set A.

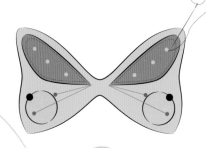

3 Lay out the two wing pieces from set B. Pin in place the decorative large dots and flower shapes. Blanket stitch around the large dots and use the diagrams as a reference to stitch the flowers in place.

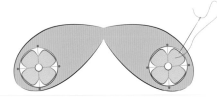

4 With wrong sides together, and using two strands of matching thread, blanket stitch around the outer edge of butterfly wings set B.

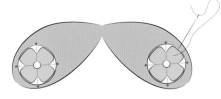

30

5 Place wing set A on top of wing set B.

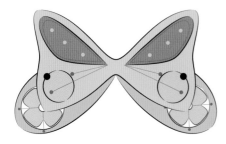

6 Pinch the middle of the wings so they 'stand up' add a few stitches to hold them in place.

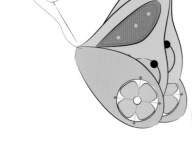

7 Take approx. 60cm (24") of thin velvet ribbon and stitch the centre of the ribbon to the middle of the wings set B. Knot the ends of the ribbon.

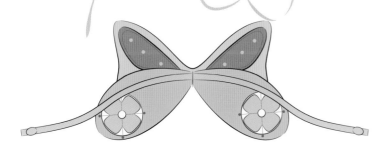

These are **scissors**.

We cut paper and cloth with scissors.

Mother uses this **scoop**

to take flour out of the

b___ lik___

into th___

(scoops ___)

See Bob ride his **scooter**

(scooters)

Our side won because we had

Summer

apron

you will need

- 38cm x 33cm (15″x 13″) fabric for apron
- x1 6mm (¼″) button
- Perle thread for button loop
- General sewing supplies

* 5mm seam allowance included

* templates on page 110

pocket

1 Cut a piece of fabric for the pocket that measures approx. 8cm x 12cm (3″x 5″).

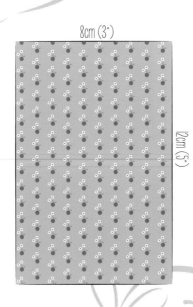

8cm (3″)

12cm (5″)

2 With right sides of the fabric together, fold it in half and trace one pocket on to the fabric.

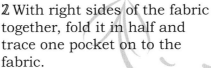

3 Machine stitch all the way around the pocket along the traced line, leaving open where indicated along the top edge. Cut out the pocket leaving a tiny seam allowance.

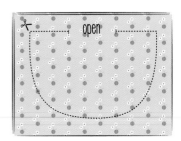

open

4 Clip the curves, turn right side out and press. Hand stitch the opening closed.

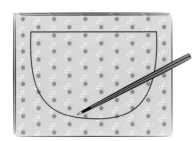

are taught.

...ms.)

...s.

cloth with sciss...

coop

of t... can.

...in...

(sc...

se we had

...

er of points.

minute of the game.

d scoring)

sea

sea

The boat ...

The **sea** is ...

The water ...

seaso...

sea...

Winter and ...

Spring and a ...

Which **seaso...**

...e se...

...a sea...

...ts s...

sec-ona

second

Bob is the fi...

Mary is the s...

n...

seesaw

apron

1 Cut four pieces for the ties that measure – 4"x ¾" (10cm x 1.3cm).

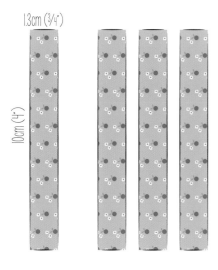

1.3cm (¾")

10cm (4")

2 Take one piece and press in a tiny amount on one short end.

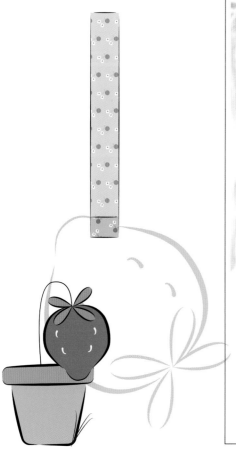

3 With wrong sides together, fold the piece in half lengthwise, and press. Open it out and press the long raw edges in to the centre crease and press. Now fold the piece in half again and press. Top stitch along this edge.

4 Repeat with the remaining three tie pieces.

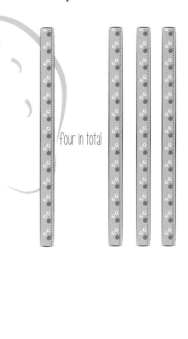

four in total

5 Pin the raw end of both ties in place as shown.

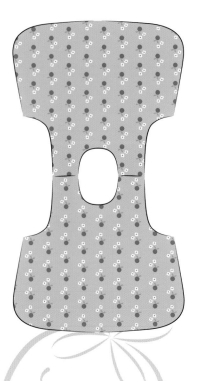

6 With right sides together, place two apron pieces together and machine stitch all the way around, leaving open where indicated along the bottom edge and making sure to catch the raw end of the ties in the stitching.

8 With the two remaining apron pieces, machine stitch across the shoulder seams.

10 Hand stitch the apron front to the back along the remaining shoulder seam. Tie up the ties in a bow on both sides of the apron.

11 Stitch a 6mm (¼") button in place on the top of the shoulder opposite the loop.

open

9 Open out and press. Using a matching Perle thread, Stitch one small button loop in one shoulder seam. Now machine stitch the rest in the same way as for step 6.

7 Clip the corners and curves and turn right side out, hand stitch the opening closed and press well. Machine top stitch the pocket in place around the curved edge, to the front of the apron.

headscarf

1 Cut a piece of fabric 40cm x 15cm (16"x 6"). With right sides together, fold the fabric for the scarf in half and cut out two on the fold.

2 With right sides together, machine stitch all the way around the headscarf, leaving open where indicated. Clip corners and curves, turn right side out and press.

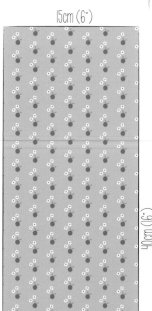

15cm (6")

40cm (6")

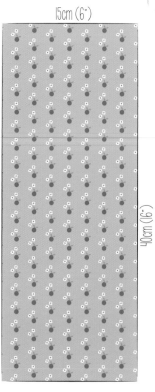

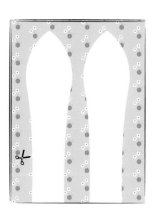

open

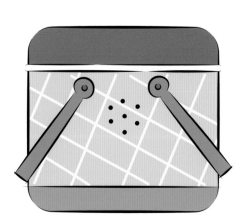

42

3 Hand stitch the opening closed. Wrap the headscarf around Marmalade's head and tie in a knot.

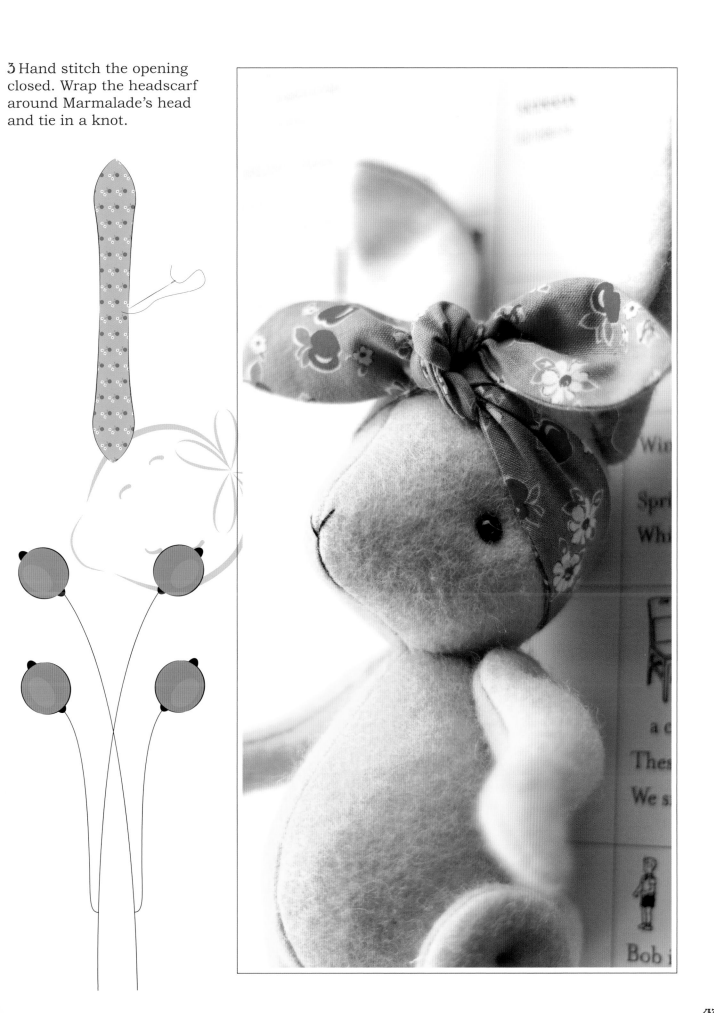

basket

.you will need.

- . 28cm x 15cm (11" x 6") aqua felt for basket and handle
- . 23cm x 15cm (9" x 6") iron on interfacing
- . x2 6mm (¼") buttons
- . Brown embroidery thread
- . Sewing machine thread to match the felt
- . General sewing supplies

✱ 3mm (⅛") seam allowance included

✱ templates on page 112

1 Using the diagrams as a reference, and two strands of brown thread, embroider in back stitch along both long sides of one basket piece.

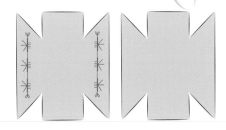

right side

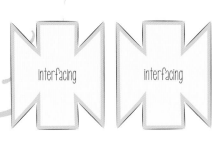

wrong side

2 Cut two pieces of iron on interfacing slightly smaller than the pattern piece. Iron the interfacing to the wrong side of both pattern pieces.

3 Place the two basket pieces wrong sides together and using a tiny 3mm (⅛") seam allowance, machine stitch all the way around the pieces.

4 Bring the pointed corners together so they are behind the rectangular end pieces. Add a few stitches to hold.

7 Hand stitch the ends of the handle in place inside the centre of the basket side.

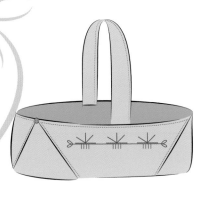

5 Stitch a tiny button in place where the points meet as decoration.

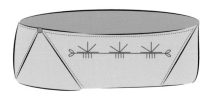

6 Fold the handle piece in half lengthwise and machine top stitch.

strawberries

. 10cm x 7cm (4"x 3")
  strawberry red wool felt
  for each strawberry
. 5cm x 5cm (2"x 2")
  green wool felt for the
  strawberry leaves
. Light brown embroidery
  thread for seeds
. Embroidery thread to
  match the felt
. Toy fill
. General sewing supplies

* 3mm (⅛") seam
   allowance included

* templates on page 116

1 Take one strawberry piece and fold it in half, machine stitch along the straight edge. Turn right side out.

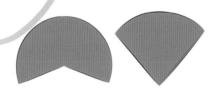

2 Using two strands of light brown embroidery thread, stitch tiny back stitches all over the surface of the strawberry (these will be the 'seeds').

3 Using two strands of matching thread to the strawberries, gather by hand around the top edge. Stuff the strawberry well, pull up the gathers and fasten off. (don't cut the thread as yet)

4 Cut out one strawberry leaf. Stitch it in place on the top of the strawberry with a tiny back stitch.

5 Make as many strawberries as you like, five fit snuggly in the basket.

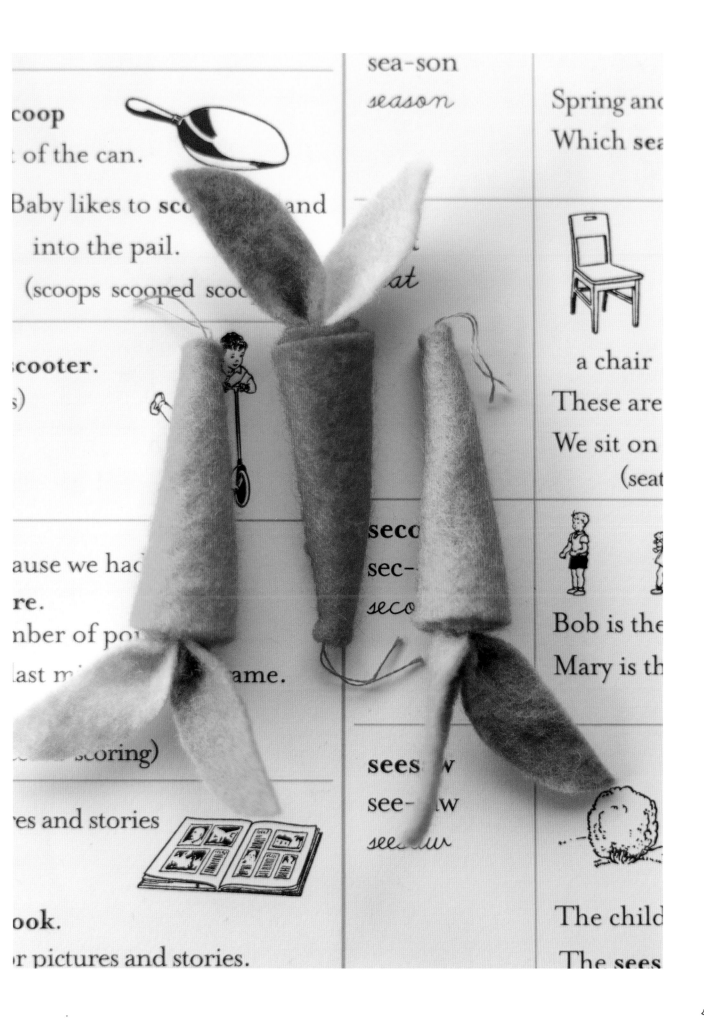

coop

t of the can.

Baby likes to sco   and

into the pail.

(scoops scooped scoo

scooter.

)

ause we had

re.

nber of po

last m   ame.

          coring)

es and stories

ook.

r pictures and stories.

sea-son

season

Spring and

Which sea

at

seco

sec-

seco

sees   w

see-   w

sees

a chair

These are

We sit on

(seat

Bob is the

Mary is th

The child

The **sees**

Autumn

dungarees

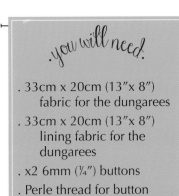

1 With right sides together, place the four dungaree pattern pieces in groups of two each having one lining and one fabric.

2 Machine stitch both shoulder seams on both groups. Open out and press the seam.

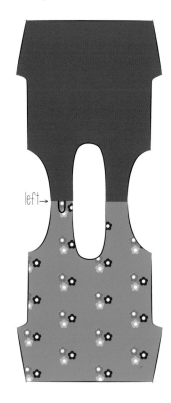

left→

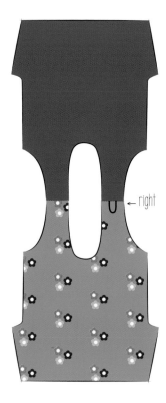

←right

3 With the lining facing upward and using a matching Perle thread, Stitch a small button loop through the top shoulder seam on the left hand side of one group and on the right hand side of the other.

4 With right sides together, machine stitch all the way around each group, leaving open where indicated along the bottom straight edge. Clip the corners and the curves, turn right side out and press. Hand stitch the opening closed.

open

open

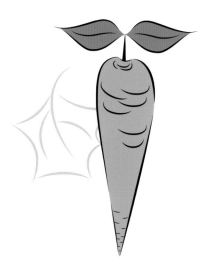

5 With the lining facing each other, hand stitch the dungarees along the gusset on both sides, leaving a small gap in the stitching on the 'button loop' side for the tail.

underarm

tail

gusset

6 Bring the gusset seam into the centre and hand stitch along the leg seams. Stitch two 6mm (¼") buttons in place on the right side of the front shoulder straps. Turn up the cuffs.

53

blouse

.you will need.

- . 38cm x 23cm (15″x 9″) fabric for the blouse
- . x2 6mm (¼″) buttons
- . Perle thread for button loops
- . General sewing supplies

* 5mm seam allowance included

* templates on page 114

1 With right sides together, machine stitch all the way around the blouse front pieces, leaving open where indicated along the bottom straight edge. Clip the corners and curves, turn right side out and press.

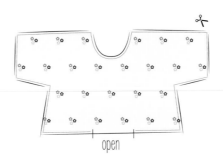

open

2 Take two of the blouse back pieces and with right sides together, machine stitch all the way around, leaving open where indicated along the bottom straight edge. Clip the corners and curves, turn right side out and press.

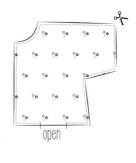

open

3 With the two remaining blouse back pieces, machine stitch down the centre back seam, open out and press. Using a matching Perle thread, Stitch two small button loops.

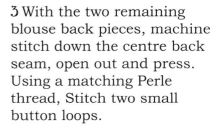

4 Now machine stitch the rest in the same way as for step 2.

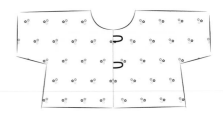

open

54

5 Hand stitch one blouse back to the blouse front along the shoulder seam, along the underarm and down the side seam.

6 Repeat with the remaining blouse back.

7 Stitch two 6mm (¼") buttons in place on the back opposite the loops.

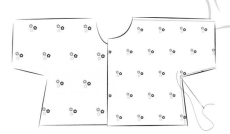

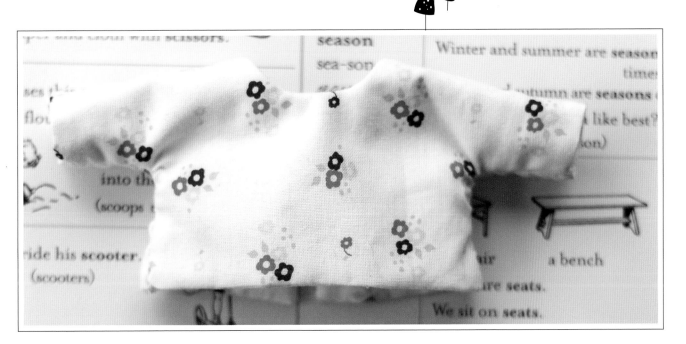

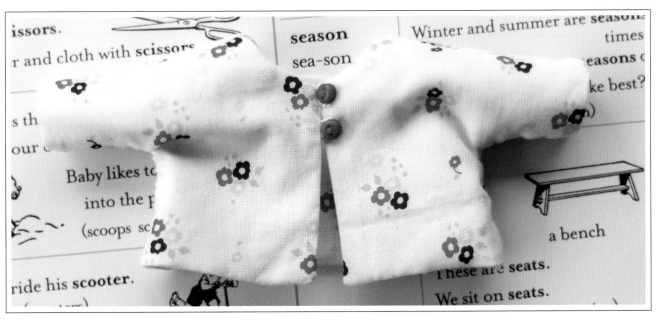

vest

1 Cut one vest piece from felt and one from fabric. Using two strands of a contrasting embroidery thread, stitch all the way around the front of the felt vest piece in blanket stitch as shown.

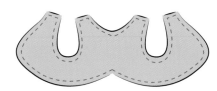

2 With right side together, stitch all the way around the vest pieces, leaving open where indicated along the neck edge. Clip curves and

corners and turn the vest right side out and press.

3 Close the gap along the neck edge. Bring one set of front and back shoulder seams together and hand stitch them in place. Repeat with the remaining two shoulder seams.

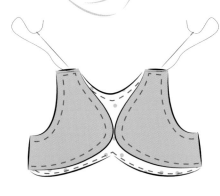

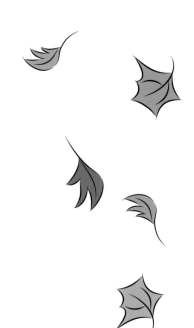

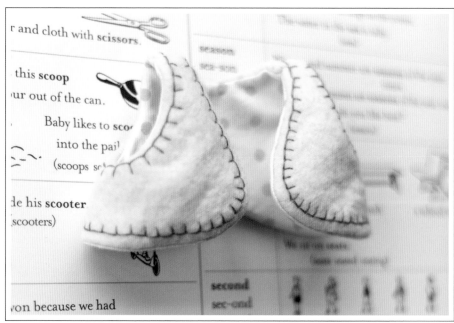

carrots

you will need

- 19cm x 10cm (7½"x 4") orange felt for the carrots
- 18cm x 4cm (7"x 1½") green felt for the carrot tops
- Embroidery thread to match the felt
- General sewing supplies

* templates on page 116

* templates on page 116

1 Take one carrot piece and beginning at one of the straight sides, roll it up tightly.

roll

2 Using two strands of matching embroidery thread, make a knot in the thread so there is a long tail in the thread. Beginning at the pointy end, blanket stitch along the raw edge of the carrot to hold. (the long end of the thread will hang out the end)

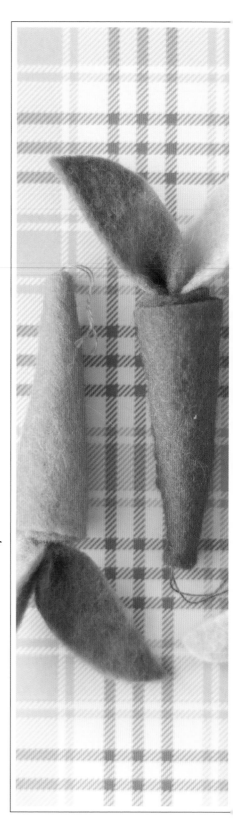

3 Cut two carrot tops from green felt and pinch at the short straight end. Add a few stitches to hold.

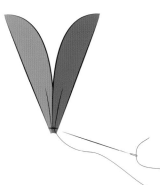

4 Bring the two carrot tops together at the pinched end and push them in to the top of the carrot. Add a few stitches to hold.

5 Make three carrots in total.

tote bag

.you will need.

- 22cm x 13cm (9"x 5")
  Beige felt for the bag
  and handles
- 22cm x 13cm (9"x 5")
  fabric for the lining
- Scraps of orange felt for
  carrot applique
- Green embroidery thread
- Sewing machine thread to
  match the Beige felt
- General sewing supplies

* 5mm seam allowance
  included

* templates on page 117

1 Fold each handle in half lengthwise and machine top stitch.

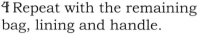

2 Using the diagrams as a reference, blanket stitch the carrots to the front of both felt bag pieces.

3 Place one lining piece and one bag piece right side together, pin the raw ends of one handle in place between the lining and bag piece along the top, straight edge. Stitch across the top edge, making sure to catch the handle ends in the stitching.

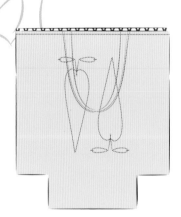

4 Repeat with the remaining bag, lining and handle.

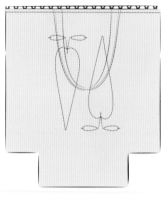

5 Open out the bag and machine stitch down both side seams, leave a small turning gap in one side of the lining. Machine stitch along the bottom edge of the bag and lining pieces. Press.

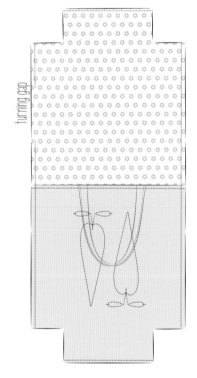

turning gap

6 Bring the side seam and the bottom seam together at the corners and stitch across. Repeat with the lining. Press.

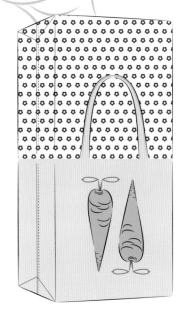

7 Turn the bag out through the gap in the lining. Hand stitch the gap closed, tuck the lining inside the bag and press well.

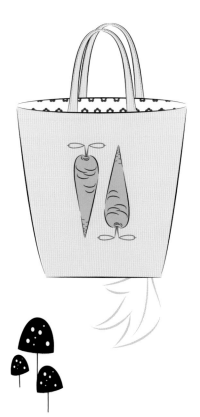

Winter

coat

.you will need.

- . 30cm x 28cm (12"x 11") aqua wool felt for coat
- . 30cm x 28cm (12"x 11") lining fabric for coat
- . 10cm x 3cm (1¼"x 4") red wool felt for flowers
- . Small scrap of deep green wool felt for flower middles
- . Hot pink, royal blue, olive green and deep green embroidery thread
- . Perle cotton for button loop
- . Small vintage button
- . Sewing machine thread to match the felt
- . General sewing supplies

* 5mm seam allowance included

* templates on page 118

1 Using the same flower as for the butterfly wings (page 109), cut out four from red felt (don't cut out the middle circle this time). Using four strands of hot pink embroidery thread, stitch the flowers in place with long back stitches, through the centre, approx. 5cm (2") up from the bottom edge of both coat fronts.

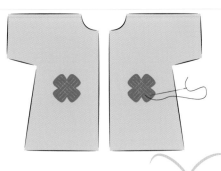

2 Repeat with coat back, using two flowers.

3 Cut out four flower middles from deep green felt, stitch them in place in the centre of each flower using blanket stitch.

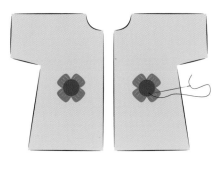

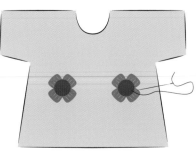

4 Using two strands of royal blue embroider thread, follow the diagrams and stitch the stems of each flower using back stitch.

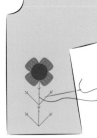

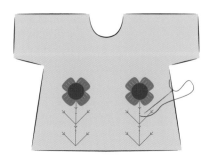

5 Stitch a row of running stitch across the front of each piece just above the flower.

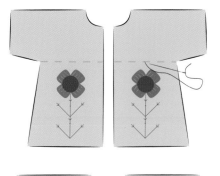

6 With right sides together, place the felt coat back together with the fabric coat back. Machine stitch all the way around, leaving open where indicated along the side edge. Clip the corners and curves and turn right side out, hand stitch the opening closed and press well.

7 Take one felt coat front and one fabric coat front. With right sides together, machine stitch all the way around, leaving open where indicated along the side edge. Clip the corners and curves, turn right side out and press.

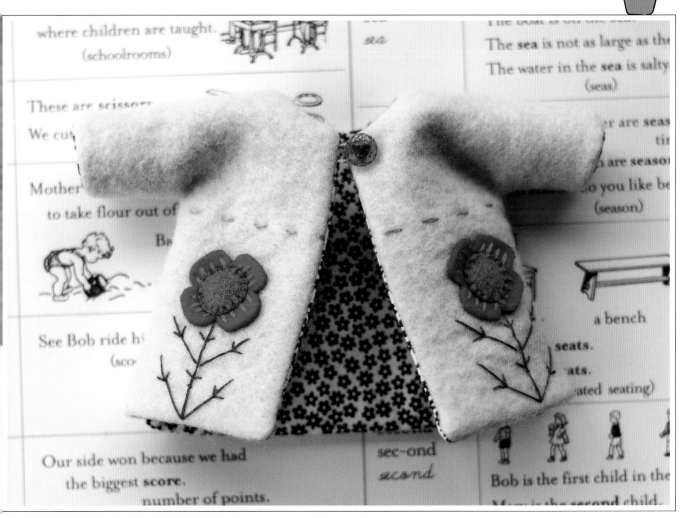

8 With the remaining felt coat front and fabric coat front, machine stitch down the centre front seam, open out and press. Using a matching Perle thread, Stitch a small button loop.

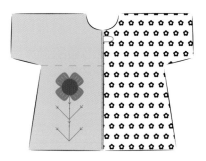

9 Now machine stitch the rest in the same way as for step 7.

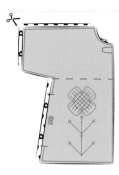

10 Hand stitch one coat front to the coat back along the shoulder seam and down the side seam.

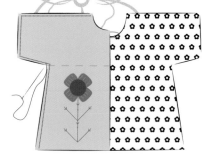

11 Repeat with the remaining coat front.

12 Stitch a small vintage button in place on the front opposite the loop.

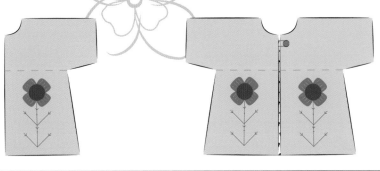

skirt

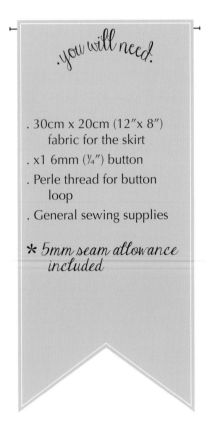

.you will need.

. 30cm x 20cm (12"x 8")
  fabric for the skirt
. x1 6mm (¼") button
. Perle thread for button
  loop
. General sewing supplies

* 5mm seam allowance
  included

1 Cut a piece for the skirt that measures 18cm x 30cm- (7"x 12"). and a piece for the waist band that measures 20cm x 2.5cm (8"x 1")

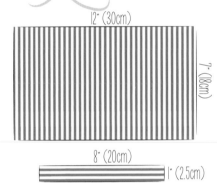

12" (30cm)

7" (18cm)

8" (20cm)   1" (2.5cm)

2 With right side together, Fold the skirt in half lengthwise. Using a scant 5mm seam allowance, machine stitch the short ends and turn the skirt right side out and press. You now have a raw edge at the top and two neatly stitched sides.

3 Machine gather along the top raw edge of the skirt, pull the gathers evenly and lay the skirt aside.

← gather →

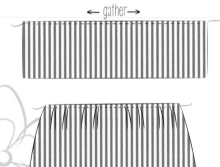

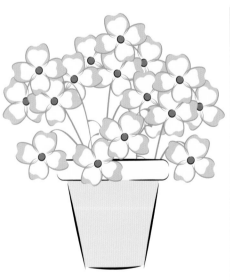

4 Take the waistband piece and with right sides of the band facing one side of the skirt, pin the band to the top raw edge of the skirt, leave approx. ½" of the band over hanging either side of the skirt, stitch the band in place adjusting gathers in the skirt as you stitch.

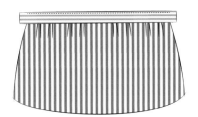

5 Press the band up and over to the inside of the skirt and hand stitch the raw edge to the inside of the skirt, tucking under the raw edge of the band as you stitch.

6 Tuck in the raw ends of the band on both ends, using Perle thread, stitch a small button loop in one end of the band.

7 Press the skirt well. Beginning at the bottom edge, hand stitch the skirt together, along the neat ends, approx. half way up.

8 Stitch a 6mm (¼") button in place on the back of the band opposite the loop.

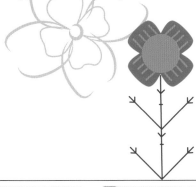

bonnet

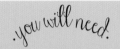

.you will need.

- . 26cm x 22cm (10"x 9") green wool felt for bonnet
- . 40cm (16") red velvet ribbon
- . x2 small wool felt pompoms
- . Sewing machine thread to match the felt
- . Embroidery thread to match the felt
- . White, Olive Green and Red embroidery thread
- . Pinking Shears
- . General sewing supplies

* *5mm seam allowance included*

* *templates on page 120*

1 Matching the symbols, bring one X and one O together and machine stitch. Repeat on the other side of one bonnet piece.

2 Repeat step 1 with the remaining bonnet piece.

76

3 Using two strands of white embroidery thread and using backstitch, stitch four snowflakes randomly over the right side of one of the bonnet pieces.

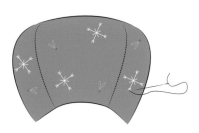

8 Gather by hand along the open raw bottom edge of the bonnet. Pull gathers so the bottom edge measures approx. 11.5cm (4½")

4 Using two strands of olive green embroidery thread and using lazy daisy stitch, stitch four groups of two leaves in the shape of a 'V' randomly around the snowflakes.

5 Using four strands of red embroidery thread, stitch groups of three French knots at the base of each 'V'

6 With wrong sides together, machine stitch along the long front edge of the bonnet.

7 Trim the front edge with Pinking Shears. Tuck the plain bonnet piece inside the embroidered one.

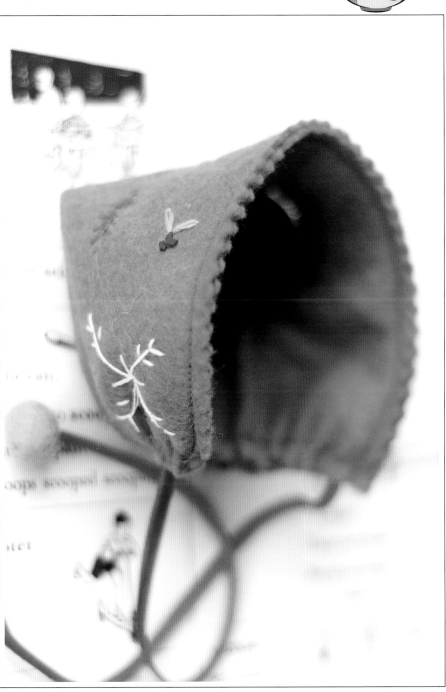

9 Cut 40cm (16") piece of velvet ribbon in half and push one end of each piece inside the opening as marked. Set your machine to zig zag and top stitch along the bottom gathered edge, making sure to catch the ends of the ribbon in the stitching.

10 Stitch a small felt pompom to the ends of the ribbon.

11 Using two strands of matching embroidery thread, blanket stitch around the ear openings.

ear openings

Bedtime

moses basket bed

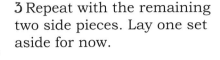

.you will need.

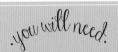

- . Large piece of paper to make side piece pattern
- . 65cm x 48cm (25½"x 19") wool felt for Moses Basket bed
- . 65cm x 48cm (25½"x 19") light weight iron on interfacing
- . 28cm x 20cm (11"x 8") fabric for inner base
- . 28cm x 20cm (11"x 8") iron on batting for inner base
- . 20cm x 12cm (8"x 5") thick cardboard for inner base.
- . Perle embroidery thread for cut out handles
- . 5cm x 5cm (2"x 2") coral felt for roses
- . 18cm x 5cm (7"x 2") peach felt for roses
- . 8cm x 6cm (3" x 2½") leaf green felt for leaves
- . 12cm x 8cm (5" x 3") willow green felt for leaves
- . Sewing machine thread to match the felt
- . Pinking Shears
- . General sewing supplies
- . Craft glue

✶ 5mm seam allowance included

✶ templates on page 121

bed

1 Fold a large piece of paper in half. Place the Moses basket bed side piece on the fold as indicated and trace. Cut out, this will be your pattern piece. From this pattern piece cut out four in felt and four from the interfacing.

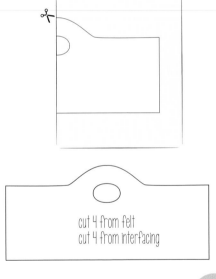

paper

cut 4 from felt
cut 4 from interfacing

2 Iron the light iron on interfacing to all pieces. Take two of the side pieces and with right sides together, stitch them down the side seams. Press the seams open.

3 Repeat with the remaining two side pieces. Lay one set aside for now.

4 Using pins as markers, divide one set of the side pieces in to four, along the long straight edge.

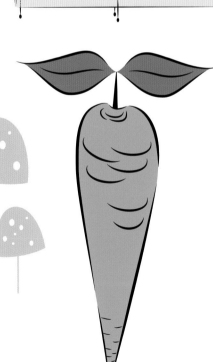

5 Do the same around the outer edge of the bed base piece.

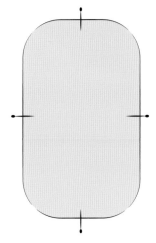

6 With right sides together, Machine stitch the side piece to the bed base, easing around the corners of the bed base and matching the pin markers in the side piece to the pins in the bed base as you stitch.

7 Use Pinking Shears to carefully trim around the bed base seam.

8 Turn right side out and press around the base seam.

9 With right sides together, stitch the remaining set of side pieces to the first set, stitching around the top edge. Use the Pinking Shears again to carefully trim around the seam.

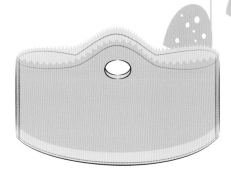

10 Turn the side pieces to the inside of the bed. Press the top edge well and top stitch around the top edge.

11 Gather lightly by hand around the inside raw straight edge of the inner side of the bed. Adjust the gathers evenly and fasten off

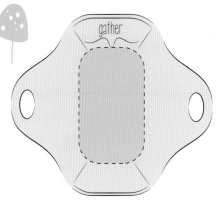

gather

12 Using one strand of Perle embroidery thread, blanket stitch around the cut out handles.

13 Using the bed base pattern as a guide, cut one piece of fabric and one piece of iron on batting approx. 2.5cm (1") larger than the pattern piece for the inner base.

14 Iron the batting to the wrong side of the fabric. Gather by hand around the outer edge of the fabric.

15 Place the thick cardboard bed base inside and pull up the gathers and fasten off.

16 Place craft glue on the wrong side of the cardboard base and carefully stick it inside the bed base.

roses

1 Cut out 2 petals from coral felt, and 10 petals from peach felt. Take one of the coral petals and with the flat edge facing the bottom, roll the petal into a spiral shape. Add a few tiny stitches along the raw edge to hold in place.

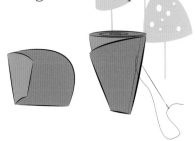

2 Use 5 peach petals, wrap each petal around the centre spiral petal, (add a few stitches to hold in place) each one being placed opposite the previous one until all 5

have been stitched. Use the remaining petals to make a second rose.

3 Take one small leaf and pinch the straight edge, add a few stitches to hold it in place. Repeat with the remaining small leaves.

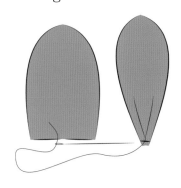

4 Follow the diagrams to stitch the roses and leaves to the outside of the bed under the handle.

sleeping bag and pillow

sleeping bag

1 With right sides together, machine stitch the top long edge of the bag piece to one long edge of the bag panel piece, Press open.

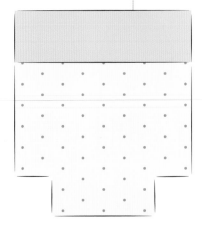

2 Repeat with the remaining bag and panel pieces.

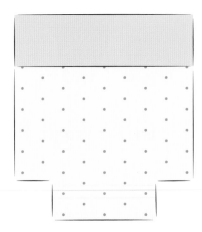

3 Use one of these as the pattern to cut two pieces for the lining and two from iron on batting.

4 Iron the batting to the wrong side of both bag pieces.

5 Using a ¼" foot on your sewing machine, top stitch diagonally across the whole piece. This will give a quilted effect. Repeat with remaining bag piece.

6 With right sides together, stitch down the side seams of the bag. Now stitch across the bottom edge of the bag.

7 Pull each corner apart so the side seam and the bottom seam match, stitch across these edges.

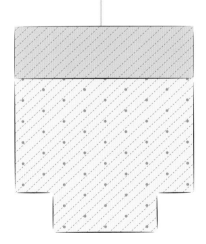

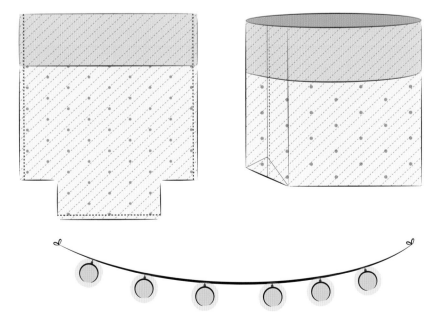

8 Repeat step 6 and step 7 to make the lining. Leave a small turning gap in one side seam.

9 With right sides together, slide the bag inside the lining. Stitch the lining to the sleeping bag around the top opening edge. Turn right side out through the gap in the lining. Press well and hand stitch the turning gap closed.

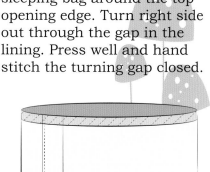

10 Take a piece of 2cm (¾") wide bias tape approx. 35cm (14") long. Turn under a neat hem on both ends and stitch in place.

11 Top stitch it in place around the opening edge of the sleeping bag, leaving a small 2.5cm (1") space in the front.

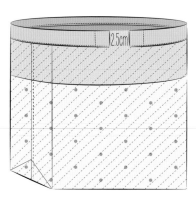

12 Take a piece of thin velvet ribbon, approx. 56cm (22") long and using a tiny safety pin, thread the ribbon through the bias tape. Knot the ends of the ribbon.

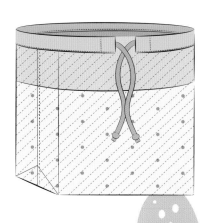

pillow

1 Using a quilting ruler, rotary cutter and mat cut the following for the pillow:

Main piece x1   - 4" x 7"
End panels x 2   - 3¼" x 7"
Batting x1   - 4" x 7"

2 Iron the batting to the wrong side of the main pillow piece. Using the ¼" foot on your sewing machine, top stitch in the same way as the sleeping bag.

3 With right sides together, stitch the long 18cm (7") side of the end panels to either long 18cm (7") end of the main piece.

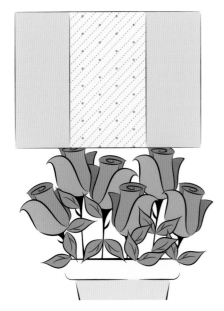

4 Fold the pillow in half, making sure the end panels are still at the end. Stitch along the seam, turn right side out and press.

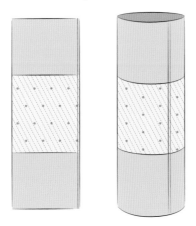

5 Fold under each raw end. Measure in approx. 2.5cm (1") and gather by hand around each end. Pull up the gathers in one end only and fasten off.

6 Stuff the pillow until it is firm and gather the remaining end in the same way as before. Fasten off.

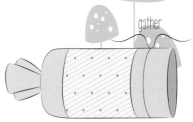

7 Cut approx. 60cm (23.5") thin velvet ribbon. Cut it in half, tie a knot in each end and tie each piece around the ends of the pillow.

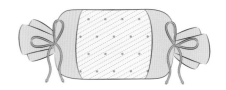

pyjamas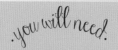

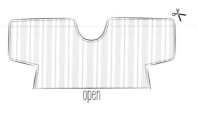

.you will need.

- . 54cm x 41cm (21"x 16") fabric for pyjamas
- . Matching Perle thread for button loops
- . x4 6mm (¼") buttons
- . 20cm (8") thin decorative elastic
- . General sewing supplies

* 5mm seam allowance included

* templates on page 125

pyjama top

1 With right sides together, machine stitch all the way around the pyjama top bodice front pieces, leaving open where indicated along the bottom straight edge. Clip the corners and curves, turn right side out and press. Press under a tiny neat edge along the open bottom edge.

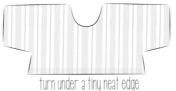

open

turn under a tiny neat edge

2 Take two of the pyjama top bodice back pieces and with right sides together, machine stitch all the way around, leaving open where indicated along the bottom straight edge. Clip the corners and curves, turn right side out and press.

open

3 Press under a tiny neat edge along the open bottom edges.

turn under a tiny neat edge

4 With the two remaining pyjama top bodice back pieces, machine stitch down the centre back seam, open out and press. Using a matching Perle thread, stitch three small button loops.

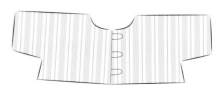

94

5 Now machine stitch the rest in the same way as for step 2.

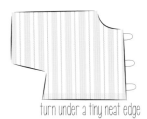

turn under a tiny neat edge

6 Cut a piece of fabric 15cm(6") x 10xm (4") for the pyjama top shirt front. With right sides together, fold the piece in half lengthwise and machine stitch down both short ends. Turn right side out and press.

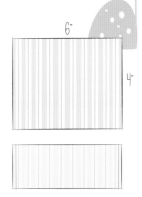

6"

4"

7 Cut two pieces of fabric 10cm (4") x 10 cm (4") for the pyjama top skirt backs. Stitch them in the same way as in step 6.

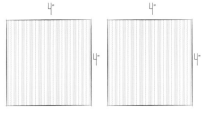

4"   4"

4"   4"

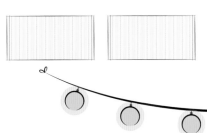

8 Gather along the top raw edge of all three skirt piece.

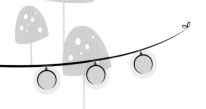

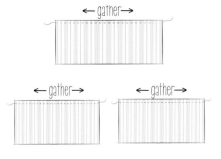

← gather →

← gather →   ← gather →

9 Tuck the gathered edge of the pyjama skirt front inside the pyjama top bodice front and hand stitch in place.

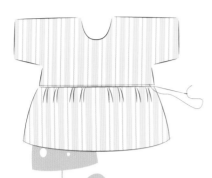

10 Repeat with the two pyjama top skirt back pieces, hand stitching them inside the pyjama top bodice back pieces.

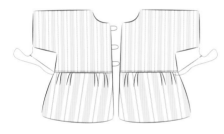

11 Hand stitch one pyjama top bodice back to the pyjama top bodice front along the shoulder seam, along the underarm and down the side seam.

12 Repeat with the remaining blouse back.

13 Stitch three 6mm (¼") buttons in place on the back opposite the loops.

14 Stitch one button to the centre front of the bodice.

pyjama trousers

1 With right sides together, stitch two of the pyjama trouser pieces all the way around, leaving open where indicated along the bottom straight edge. Clip curves and corners and turn right side out and press. Repeat with the remaining two trouser pieces. Hand stitch the opening closed.

2 Place the two trouser pieces together, and hand stitch down the two gusset seams. Leave a small gap in one gusset seam for the tail.

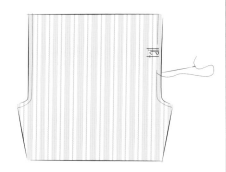

3 Bring the gusset seams to the centre front and hand stitch along the leg and crotch seams.

4 Take approx. 20cm (8") of thin decorative elastic. Using a zigzag stitch on your machine and beginning at the back seam, stitch it in place pulling it firmly as you go all the way around. Trim the excess elastic.

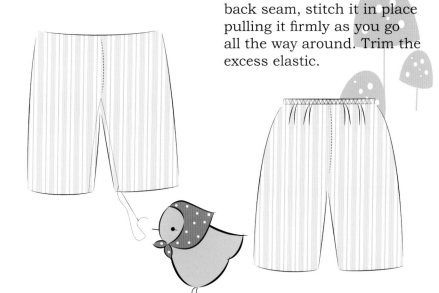

baby bunny

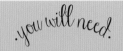

head

1 Using a tiny 3mm (⅛") seam allowance, stitch all the way around the head, leaving open where indicated at the bottom of the head.

open

2 Make a tiny snip between the ears and turn the head right side out.

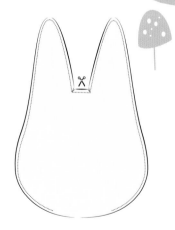

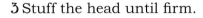

3 Stuff the head until firm.

4 Mark the position for the eyes with pins. Following the eye setting instructions on page 12, attach the English glass eyes using Gutermann Upholstery Thread to match the felt. Anchor your thread inside the stuffing in the head opening

5 Using 2 strand of black embroidery thread, stitch a tiny cross for the mouth.

body

6 Machine stitch all the way around the body, leaving open where indicated at the top straight edge.

7 Turn right side out and stuff until firm.

8 Gather by hand around the top straight open edge.

gather

9 Pull up the gathers tight and fasten off.

10 Push the top gathered edge of the body inside the opening in the head. Stitch the head on firmly.

11 Cut a piece of thin velvet ribbon approx. 20cm (8") long. Tie in a bow around the neck.

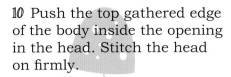

Templates

Marmalade Rabbit page 16

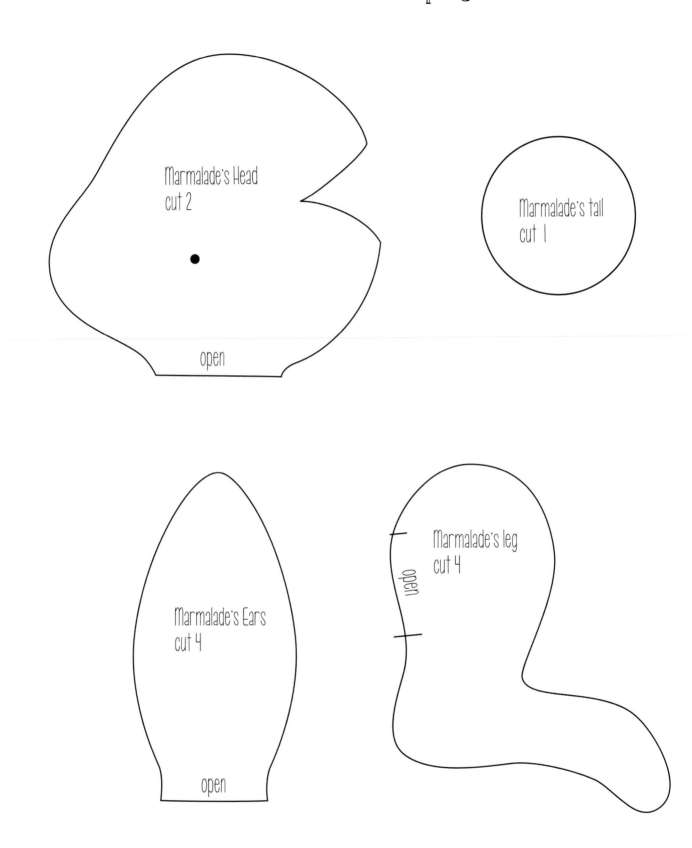

Marmalade's Head
cut 2

open

Marmalade's tail
cut 1

Marmalade's Ears
cut 4

open

Marmalade's leg
cut 4

open

templates actual size

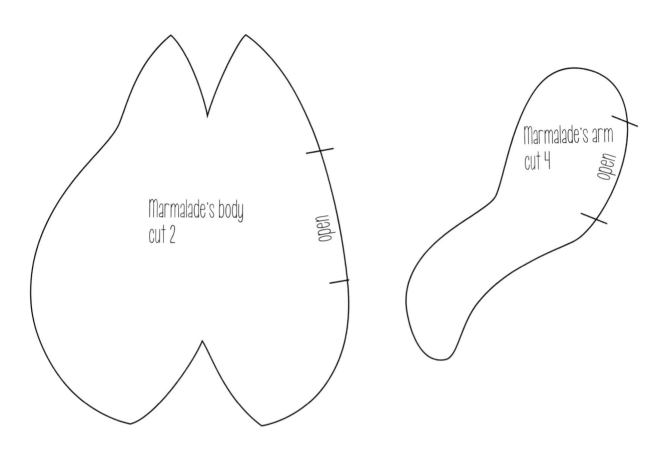

Marmalade's body
cut 2

open

Marmalade's arm
cut 4

open

Chicks page 28

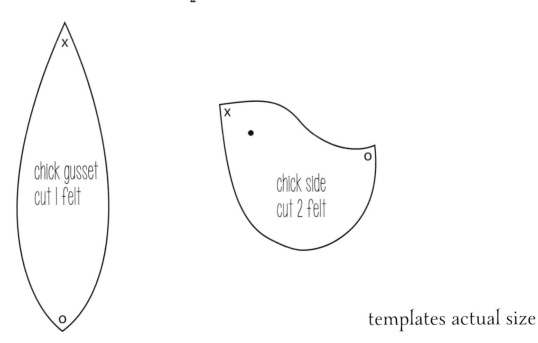

chick gusset
cut 1 felt

chick side
cut 2 felt

templates actual size

Dress page 24

dress front
cut 2 fabric

open

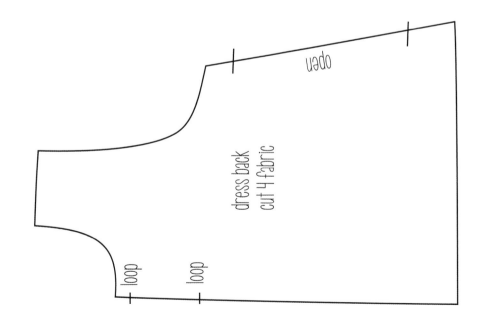

dress back
cut 4 fabric

open

loop   loop

templates actual size

Butterfly Wings page 30

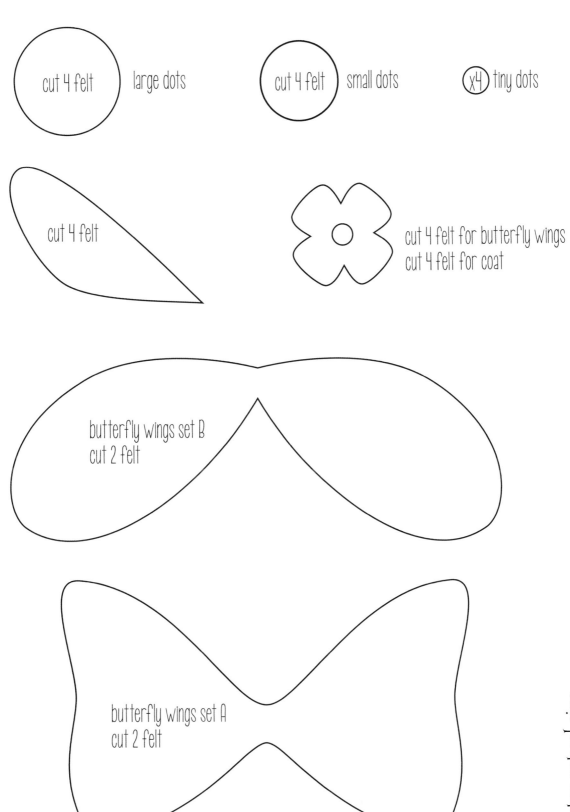

cut 4 felt   large dots

cut 4 felt   small dots

x4 tiny dots

cut 4 felt

cut 4 felt for butterfly wings
cut 4 felt for coat

butterfly wings set B
cut 2 felt

butterfly wings set A
cut 2 felt

templates actual size

Apron page 36

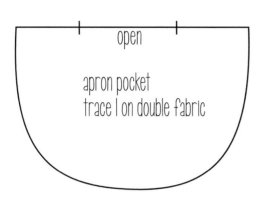

open

apron pocket
trace 1 on double fabric

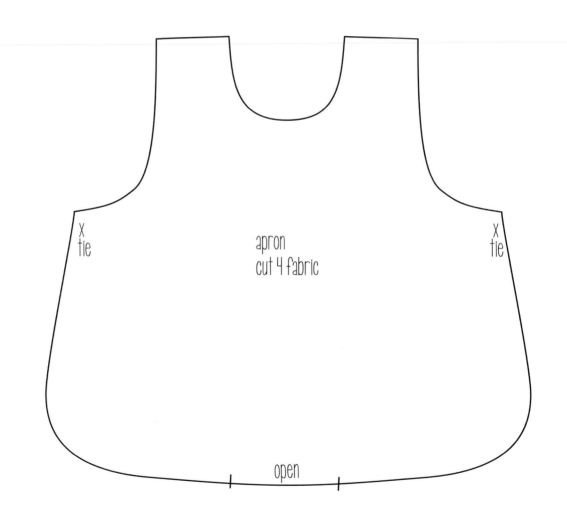

X
tie

apron
cut 4 fabric

X
tie

open

templates actual size

Headscarf page 42

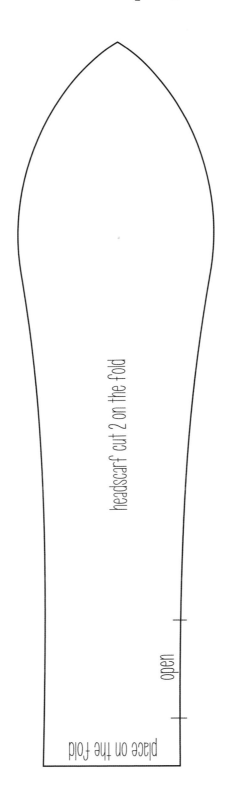

headscarf cut 2 on the fold

open

place on the fold

templates actual size

Basket page 44

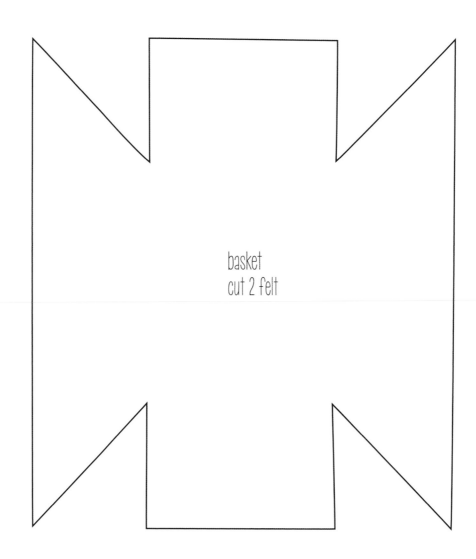

basket
cut 2 felt

basket handle cut 1 felt

templates actual size

Dungarees page 52

underarm

gusset

gusset

dungarees
cut 2 fabric
cut 2 lining

open

templates actual size

Blouse page 54

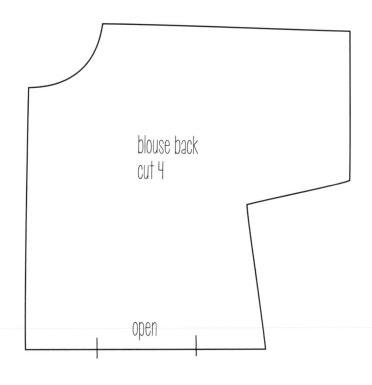

blouse back
cut 4

open

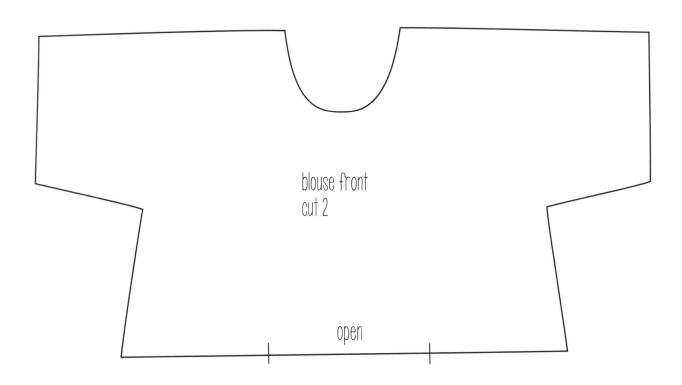

blouse front
cut 2

open

templates actual size

Vest page 58

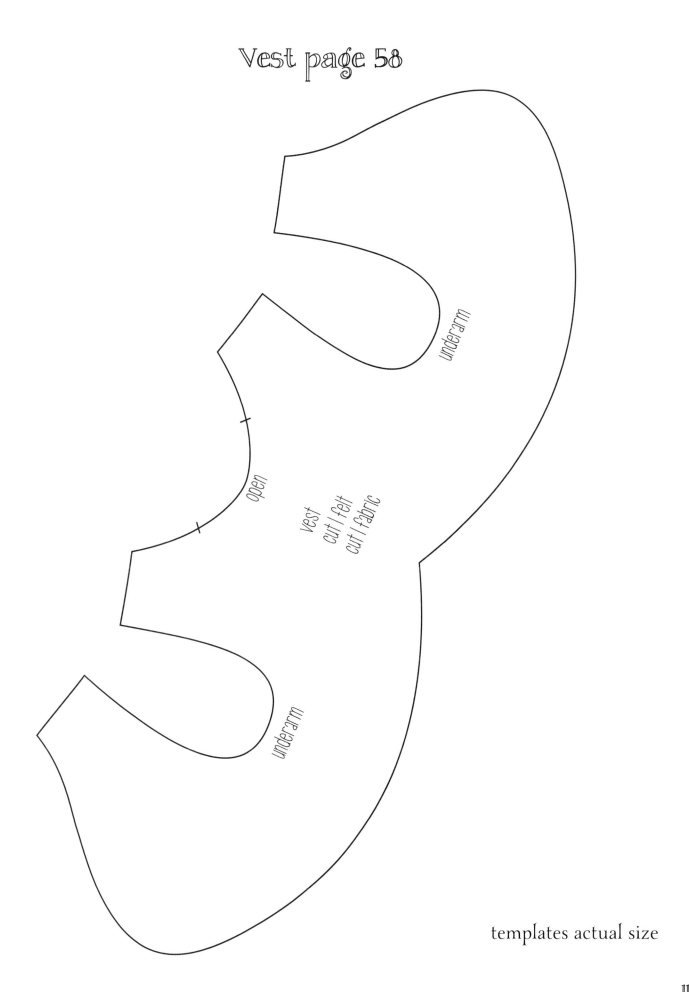

underarm

open

vest
cut 1 felt
cut 1 fabric

underarm

templates actual size

Carrots page 60

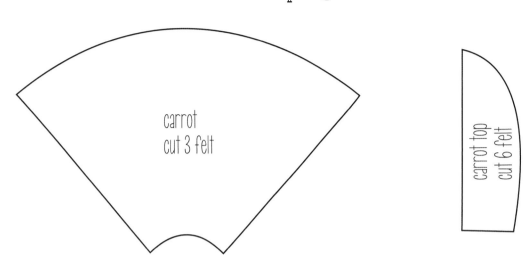

carrot
cut 3 felt

carrot top
cut 6 felt

Strawberries page 46

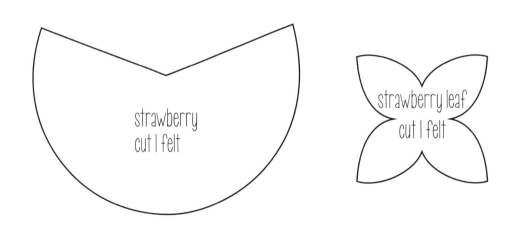

strawberry
cut 1 felt

strawberry leaf
cut 1 felt

templates actual size

Tote Bag page 62

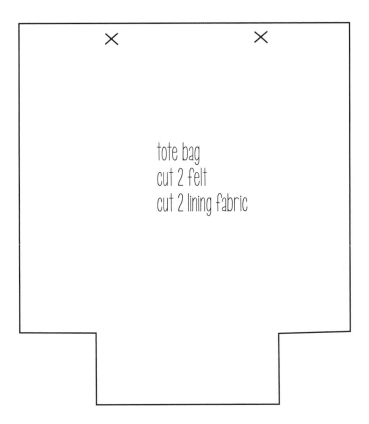

tote bag
cut 2 felt
cut 2 lining fabric

tote bag handle cut 2 felt

carrot cut 4 felt

templates actual size

Coat page 68

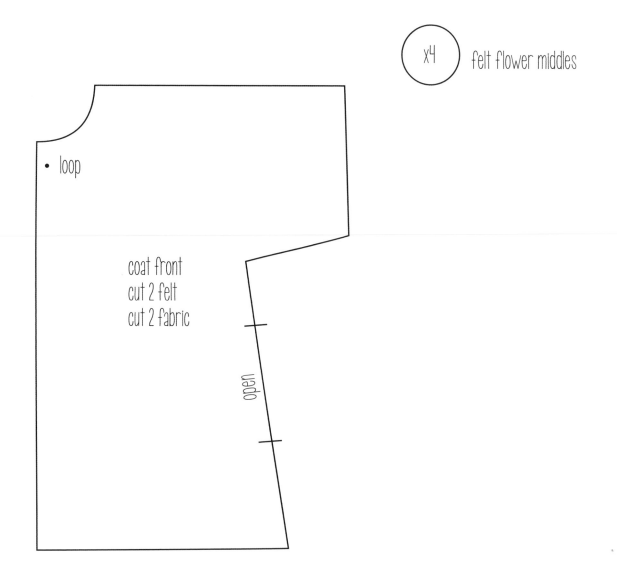

x4 felt flower middles

- loop

coat front
cut 2 felt
cut 2 fabric

open

templates actual size

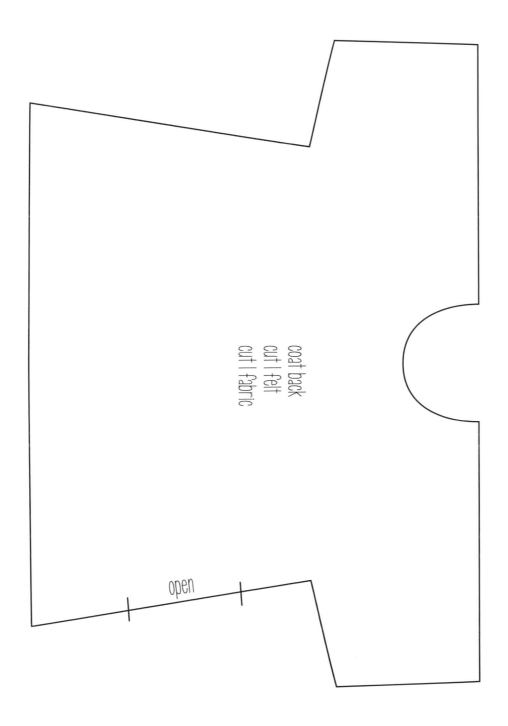

coat back
cut 1 felt
cut 1 fabric

open

templates actual size

Bonnet page 76

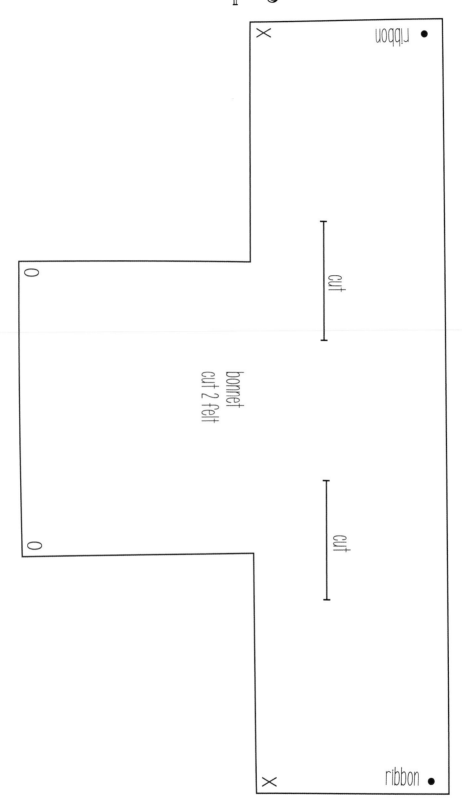

bonnet
cut 2 felt

cut

cut

ribbon ●

ribbon ●

templates actual size

Moses Basket Bed page 84

place on the fold of a large piece of paper
to make the pattern piece

moses basket bed side
cut 4 felt
cut 4 light weight iron on interfacing

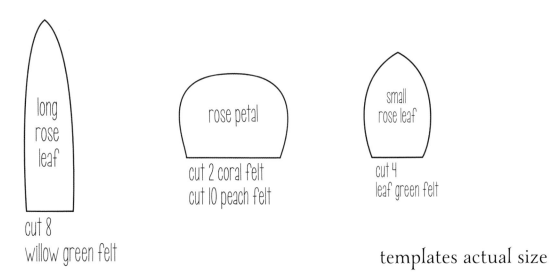

long
rose
leaf

cut 8
willow green felt

rose petal

cut 2 coral felt
cut 10 peach felt

small
rose leaf

cut 4
leaf green felt

templates actual size

moses basket bed base
cut 1 felt
cut 1 light weight iron on interfacing

templates actual size

moses basket bed cardboard template
cut 1

templates actual size

templates actual size

Sleeping Bag page 88

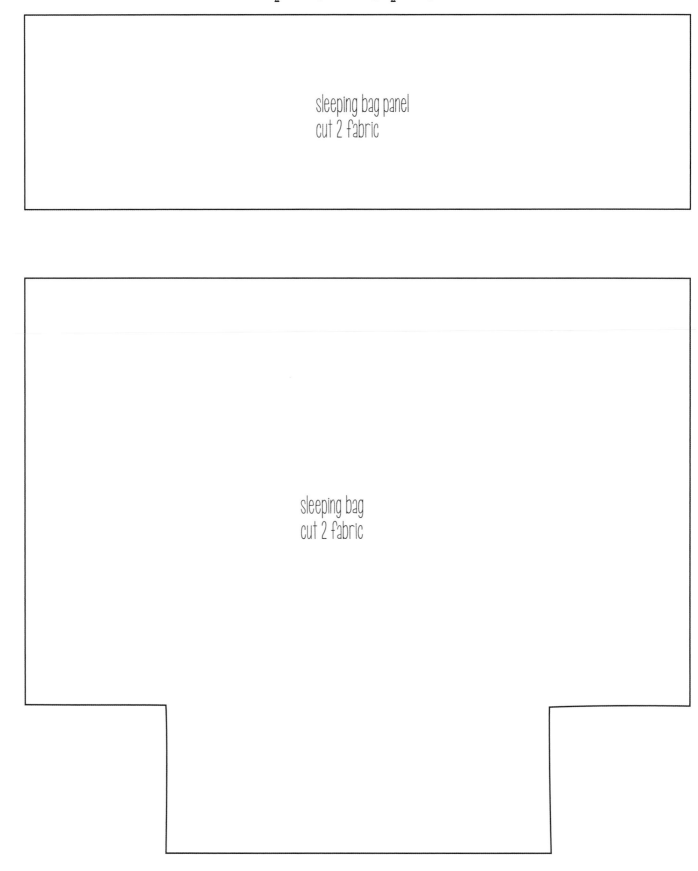

sleeping bag panel
cut 2 fabric

sleeping bag
cut 2 fabric

Pyjamas page 94

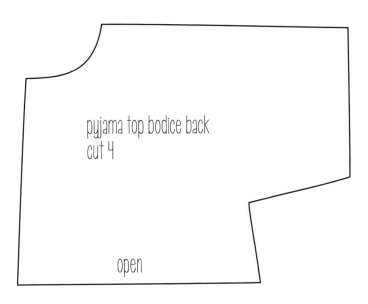

pyjama top bodice back
cut 4

open

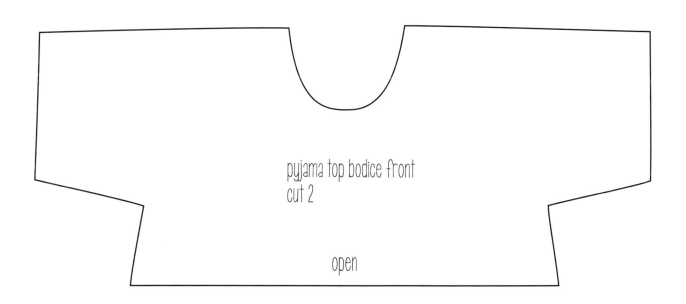

pyjama top bodice front
cut 2

open

templates actual size

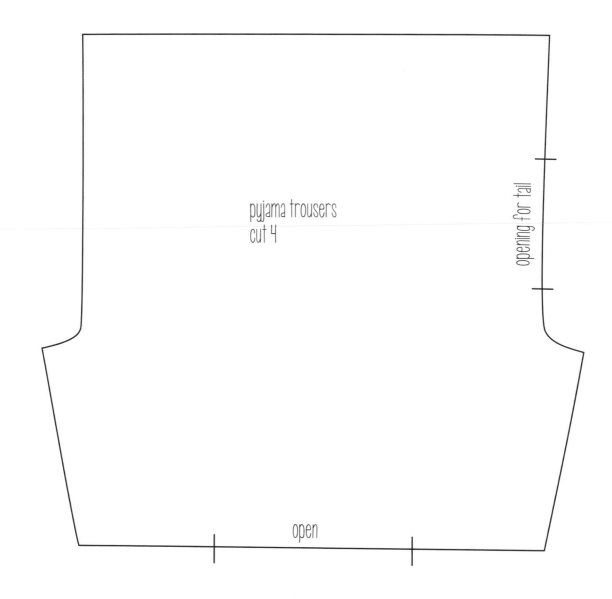

pyjama trousers
cut 4

opening for tail

open

templates actual size

Baby Bunny page 98

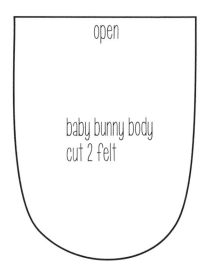

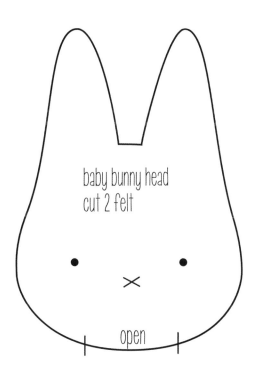

templates actual size

Suppliers

felt

Winterwood
www.winterwoodtoys.com.au

fabric

L'uccello
www.luccello.com.au

linen

The Fabric Store
www.wearethefabricstore.com

eyes

Bear Essence
www.bearessence.com.au

pompoms

L'uccello
www.luccello.com.au

embroidery thread

Cosmo Embroidery Thread
www.etsy.com

buttons

Vintage
www.etsy.com and my own collection

6mm (¼")
www.etsy.com